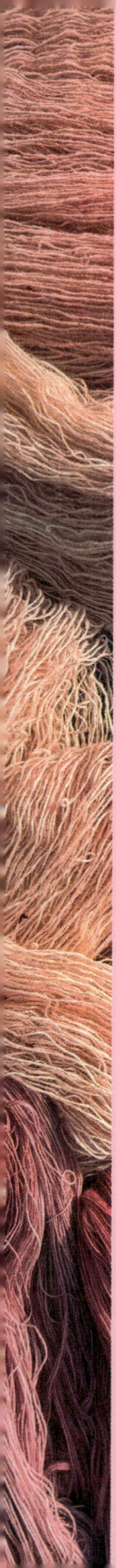

AITOR SARAIBA lives and works in a stone cabin in the valleys of Cantabria, northern Spain. He has been working in drawing, textile art and ceramics for two decades, and his work has been exhibited all over the world, from Los Angeles to Tokyo, including Portugal, Italy, the United Kingdom, Africa and several cities in Spain.

Aitor's textile work explores different traditional techniques and brings them into his own unique world. He has revived traditional wool-working processes with his flock of sheep in the mountains where he lives, uses natural dyes with silver, and employs all manner of darning and mending techniques to create stunning, unique artworks.

In *Embroider, mend and sew*, Aitor explores his textile process, wherein personal history and creativity intertwine.

Find Aitor online: www.aitorsaraiba.com
and on Instagram @aitorsaraiba

Embroider, mend and sew

First published in the UK in 2027 by
Search Press Limited
Wellwood, North Farm Road,
Tunbridge Wells, Kent TN2 3DR

1 2 3 4 5 6 7 8 9 10

This edition is published by arrangement
with Editorial GG.

Original title *Cose, zurce y borda*, published
by Editorial GG, Barcelona, Spain, 2024.

English translation from the original Spanish
by Tankerton Translations.

ISBN: 978-1-80092-456-7
ebook ISBN: 978-1-80093-402-3

Bookmarked Hub
For further ideas and inspiration, and to join our free online community, visit www.bookmarkedhub.com

Publishers' notes
The Publishers and author can accept no responsibility for any consequences arising from the information, advice or instructions given in this publication.

For errata, please visit our website (www.searchpress.com) or the Bookmarked Hub (www.bookmarkedhub.com).

GPSR information can be found at
www.searchpress.com
Printed in China, RRD062026.

FSC www.fsc.org MIX Paper | Supporting responsible forestry FSC® C144853

Embroider, mend and sew

Aitor Saraiba

Search Press

This book is dedicated to my mother,
who taught me to sew.

Let
love
in.

Contents

contigo
soy
yo

Introduction

It has taken me more than 20 years to create this book. I knew how to thread a needle before I learned to read and write, and am lucky enough to have grown up in a family where clothes were mended. Sewing formed part of the everyday life of the neighbourhood, where people sat in their doorways to enjoy the cooler air, while dark winter afternoons were spent next to the fire with my mother and sister.

Sewing, neighbourhood life, mending and repairing for pure survival, using whatever was to hand, zero waste, my grandfather's vegetable garden and the eggs our neighbour gave us… These are the foundations of my childhood in a place in the Spanish region of La Mancha that time has passed by and left in a forgotten corner of history.

These unwavering principles and foundations have shaped much of my work. Over the past 20 years, I have written books, made ceramics, drawn and painted, taken photographs and shot videos. All of them are imbued with something of this, of the place where I grew up, where I learned to sew. Textile art has always formed part of my work. It has taken me a long time to share what I really wanted to say through my textile work, but now, with my life completely devoted to this art, the public has given me their warmth and affection.

'With you, I am myself'

'Be brave, but above all, be free.'

This is a very simple book, but I have dedicated many hours to it. When the idea of writing it first came to me, my goal was that anyone who embraced it would feel what inspired me, what drove me on with every stitch; gaining other perspectives on the small but vast world of sewing. But above all, I wanted them to be free. This is its great purpose: to bring freedom to every corner of daily life, especially in creative terms, and from there, to discover the most beautiful thing a human being can ever know: oneself.

This book is also dedicated to all those people, near and far, who, through social media, encourage me to keep doing the most beautiful job in the world: where every stitch is imbued with emotions, fears and desires.

I also want to thank everyone who has come to my workshops in Japan, Spain, Mexico and Portugal. No matter where you come from, you are all incredible people, and I hope you will never cease to illuminate my path. Thank you.

'Infancy is the place where we spend the rest of our lives.'

Rosa Montero

TEXTILE
projects

30 metros

Scapular

Few places have been so etched into my body and soul as Mexico. I lived in this country for several years, and since then, an invisible umbilical cord has bound me to it, and its colours, flavours and sounds. Mexico takes hold of you the moment you set foot in the country.

It is a place where a number of textile techniques or customs that have practically disappeared are still alive and well. And it is precisely in everyday life that textiles often play an important role in a country's culture. Among the many things that have piqued my curiosity, such as backstrap looms, Michoacán embroidery, traditional costumes, their altars and huarache sandals, I have always been inspired by scapulars – textile amulets that serve as tiny portable shrines, the repository of people's individual beliefs and desires. The scapular is a small accessory that anyone can afford to buy or make.

Whatever your beliefs, textiles have been linked to worship since the beginning of time. Many talismans fashioned from fabric can be found throughout history and across different cultures. Here, I invite you to create your own scapular; let your imagination run free in terms of colours, textures and small magical symbols, and create something that is genuinely full of emotion.

I sewed onto my scapular little things I had kept because they held a special meaning for me: a shell, a little charm, a diamond-shaped mother-of-pearl button, to name but a few.

I always find a lot of inspiration on my travels. In places like Mexico, it comes to me through all my senses.

DEWHURST'S
SYLKO
THREE
SHELLS
SILK SUBSTITUTE
MACHINE 40 TWIST
J. & P. COATS
SUPER
SHEEN
MACHINE TWIST
40
100 YARDS

People sometimes tell me they would like to take part in one of my workshops and recreate one of my pieces. Many are surprised or even disappointed to discover that the materials I use are personal, perhaps found during my travels or inherited over time, and that most of the things I use are practically unique. I am always surprised that they are disappointed, rather than inspired to search through their own drawers for forgotten treasures that can breathe life into their own work. It is never long, however, before they start to realize that it is in uniqueness that value lies.

My workshops are less about technique and more about training your eye to spot useful items at flea markets, or appreciating the value of old bits and pieces long forgotten by your family. What I try to share in these workshops is a way of being in the world.

I learned some of my favourite techniques in Chiapas and Oaxaca, two places where textile art is present on every corner.

Altars, amulets, celebrations…
Mexico provides inspiration even in the tiniest of things. Traces of this country where I lived can always be seen in my work.

Instructions

1. Cut two pieces of fabric measuring approximately 6 × 7cm (2½ × 2¾in). These will form the front and the back of the scapular.

2. Find some ribbon, lace or a strip of fabric that is approximately 1cm (½in) wide and the right length to hang your scapular around your neck.

3. Appliqué a heart onto the base fabric. You will find a template among the illustrations at the end of the book (see page 202).

4. Sew the front and back together, sandwiched around a piece of thicker fabric. This could be a scrap of an old towel or blanket – something that will bulk out your scapular. Sew the ribbon to the top of the front piece before sewing the layers together.

5. Decorate with buttons, pendants, shells – give your creativity free rein.

6. Never consider your scapular finished. There is always room to add more beads or other little treasures you find along the way.

Add more details to your scapular whenever the fancy takes you; you'll find surprising little objects that are just what you need appearing wherever you look.

NTRA. SEÑORA DEL
SAGRADO CORAZON
NIÑO JESUS
¡DETENTE! EL CORAZON DE JESUS ESTA CONMIGO!
VENGA A NOSOTROS TU REINO
¡Detente! el Corazon de Jesus esta conmigo.
¡VENGA A NOS EL TU REINO!

ABBAYE DE FLAVIGNY - BONBONS A LA ROSE
FLAVIGNY ABBEY - ROSE CANDIES FLAVORED
Sin miedo

Framed appliqué

We all have things like a sweater that we have accidentally washed at the wrong temperature, an old blanket, a felted scarf or a worn piece of fabric. You can use anything as the background for framed appliqué. This is a very simple technique, which gives great results, ideal for experimenting with layers of fabric of different textures and colours. I have great fun making these textile collages, and spend hours considering possible combinations of my scraps of fabric.

At the end of the book, in the 'Templates' section (see pages 196–203), you will find various drawings and texts that you could use for your appliqués, all based on my personal universe which often features images such as swans, hearts, hands and snakes. In many ways this technique reminds me more of painting than it does of embroidery. I choose the colours and embroider on branches, eyes and other details.

I add buttons, tiny scraps and little charms to most of my textile work and it is no different with this framed appliqué work. Feel free to sew whatever you like onto them. Maybe you are using fabric from a scarf that belonged to someone very special – could you also incorporate some buttons from clothes that they no longer wear, or an old pendant? The result could be a very beautiful, personal gift.

Textiles are full of memories: the T-shirt that takes us back to our first kiss, the feel of a garment we lost but will never forget, buttons from clothes we wore as children, whose shapes and colours we remember. The more personal the materials you use for your pieces, the more character your work will have. It is these details that breathe life into what you are making.

'Fearless'

EL CISNE
Corchetes
NEGROS

sin
miedo

piensa
con el
corazón.

'Think with your heart'

Instructions

1. Stretch a piece of fabric that you like over an embroidery hoop, which will act as the frame.

2. Find a piece of woollen fabric or similar and choose an appliqué shape (remember that a wide variety of illustrations are included at the end of the book, on pages 196–203).

3. Draw the appliqué shape onto the fabric and cut out.

4. Sew on the shape using simple or decorative stitches.

5. Embroider whichever parts of the design you choose.

6. Add small remnants, buttons, rice stitches or charms to your work.

7. Your framed appliqué is ready to hang.

Feel free to decide which parts you want to embroider and which you want to cover with appliqué. Hopefully this book and its photos will spark your creativity.

Sin
miedo

Amor eterno

amoR

In this collection of framed appliqué work, you can see the different textures, buttons, fabrics, words and colours I used to bring the series to life.

Amor

Whenever you can, use matte cotton or woollen yarn for your appliqué. This will give a more uniform finish.

Let
love
in.

Boro

Darning and mending are among the first things that come to mind when I think back to the sewing that took place around me throughout my childhood. When I was a boy, my mother used to mend the knees of my trousers to make them last longer. I remember that some parts were stiffer than others because of the accumulation of patches, while the fabric itself wore thin and became easy to tear.

I also remember the rough stitches my grandfather made on a leather chair that he mended repeatedly. It was a sewing stitch that had more to do with survival than with technique or aesthetics.

Those stitches I saw my mother and grandfather making had a great influence on my eventual approach to sewing. For me, this sewing from necessity ignited an urge to do it myself, an urge beyond aesthetics; aesthetics that were kindled among the scraps.

At the age of 20, I hand-sewed a piece measuring 7m (7½yd) in length and almost 3m (3¼yd) in height. It was made from fabrics I had found discarded or left behind. They were in shades of brown and cream that people felt were dated in the fast-paced Noughties, when the thrown-away fabric smelled of the pre-digital age that everyone seemed to want to forget.

I sewed many hours a day for six months to create this piece, but I never felt it was finished; instead, one day I thought it was time to set it aside and throw myself into something new.

Those stitches I worked at the age of 20 were inspired by the mending of my grandfather and the making-do of my mother. Since then, like a spectre with its eyes always upon me, that piece has been the satellite around which the rest of my work has orbited.

About 15 years passed between making that piece and my chance discovery of the Japanese art of *boro*. There are many writings in Japanese philosophy that tell of turning flaws into virtues, into something beautiful – not hiding them, but rather showing them proudly as the scars of war, which is life itself. My knowledge of Japanese philosophy is very limited, so I will not go into that subject in depth, but I would invite anyone reading this to investigate further the extensive body of literature that exists on the subject.

I have read many versions of the history of *boro* (which translates as 'rag'), some of which are closer to the truth than others. Most of them agree that *boro* originated in northern Japan, where winters are cold, a place where, at the end of the nineteenth century, the country was in something akin to the Middle Ages in the West. Social classes were very marked, and poverty and scarcity was rife. At that time, as in many other parts of the world, there was a need to cobble together fabrics from pieces of other textiles that were no longer being put to good use.

I have travelled to Japan on many occasions and spent a great deal of time researching *boro*, but it was not until my third visit to the country that I truly understood its meaning. On a sunny winter morning in Kyoto, in an antique furniture and ceramics shop, I saw on a hanger a kimono, which had survived time and death. It was tattered, patched and mended with survival stitches (see page 76). I froze when I saw it. I had seen hundreds of photos and videos of similar pieces, and had tried to emulate them or something very similar, but this was the first time I had seen such a thing in person. That kimono, that fragile corpse of fabric, transported me to misery, decay, scarcity of resources, need, deprivation, cold, poverty; to my mother and my grandfather. I stood in front of it for a long time, not daring to touch even the exorbitant price tag that hung from it.

大正8年

Indigofera tinctoria, black henna (used for dyer's indigo), is one of my favourite plants, and its unmistakable indigo blue colour has inspired much of my work.

This photo shows the free stitches I used to make a *boro* blanket, using fabrics, which I had previously stamped using block printing.

It was only when the shop assistant came over and asked me in English if I knew what I was looking at that I was jolted out of my reverie. I replied that I did, but I still wanted her to tell me everything she knew about it. She did so, with a sobriety, elegance and careful precision that is rarely seen outside Japan.

After I had left the shop, I spent the rest of the day pondering on the flood of emotions I had felt when I had seen the kimono. I could not stop thinking about its stitches, its intense indigo colour, its patches and its layers of fabric, each one glowing like an ember. I did the conversion again and again, calculating its price in euros. Two days later, I went back and bought it. I returned to my hotel and laid it out on the bed, looking at it like you might look at an injured puppy lying in the road after a car accident. A heavy, burning tear rolled down my cheek. I folded the kimono up again, imitating the shop assistant as best I could and packed it safely away.

Boro is a technique in which indigo is the predominant colour because it was one of the colours available to even the poorest people in Japan. Bright, striking colours had different destinies as they were used only by people with power and money.

Indigo is antibacterial and fire-resistant. When garments are dyed with this plant, their fibres become stronger and thicker, so it is not surprising that the less well-off chose this dye to make their clothes last longer.

There is a big difference between *boro* and *sashiko*, another type of decorative Japanese sewing. *Sashiko* was used to strengthen and reinforce specific parts of garments, not only to protect against the cold, but also to bolster more vulnerable areas, such as the knees, elbows or shoulders, which bore the brunt of everyday work.

Sashiko is based on specific stitches and patterns, while in *boro* the stitches are free, worked solely to join fabrics together and construct a fabric that will later be used to make a garment or patch another one.

Instructions

1. Select fabrics made from natural fibres in a variety of sizes.
2. Draw different patterns and phrases on the fabrics you have chosen. You can find inspiration in the 'Templates' section of the book (see pages 196–203).
3. First work on the pieces that you want to feature as appliqué or embroidery.
4. Once your pieces are ready, join them together with a freestyle running stitch (see page 185).
5. You can continue joining pieces of fabric to your work.
6. You can use it as a bedspread, blanket or wall-hanging.

Silencio
Let love in.
oak.

Heart pin cushion

You sometimes end up with lots of fabric offcuts that can look too small to ever be used in a project. In reality, every scrap, however tiny, can be put to use sooner or later.

I invite you to make a pin cushion for your own pins and needles with those scraps you thought could no longer be of any use.

The process is very simple. The following pages feature a series of photographs to help you follow the steps visually, to make this project and inspire many future ones. You will follow the same steps for the mini throws, which feature later in the book (see page 87).

Instructions

1. Select your fabrics.
2. Use the heart in the 'Templates' section on page 199 to draw a heart on your background fabric.
3. Arrange the fabrics however you like, covering the whole of the background material.
4. Sew together using your favourite stitches and add buttons or little decorations.
5. Cut a second heart for the back piece, sew the hearts together, leaving a small gap for stuffing, then stuff and sew up the gap. Your heart pin cushion is complete.

1

2

3

4

5

Forest dwellers

I have always considered myself an animist, holding the belief that all things have a soul. I am inspired to create these little creatures using the small scraps that people give me because they think they have no further use, as well as with remnants from my own textile work. As I create them, stitch by stitch, I feel their souls beginning to come to life.

I sew them together using any leftover thread or yarn that I find in my sewing box. I like using embroidery thread or wool as it gives the forest dwellers more texture. It doesn't take much thread to bring your little creatures to life, as they don't require much fabric.

The little wolf with the red dungarees (shown on page 64) is my favourite – you can see him in the photos accompanying me on my travels. However, most of the other creatures have been adopted along the way; I have gifted them to people who have fallen in love with them at first sight; it seemed like the best possible outcome that these little forest dwellers embark on their own adventures.

Believe me, they are good travel companions: they fit anywhere, always provide love and friendship, and love having their photos taken in their favourite places.

You will find drawings to help you make your own creatures in the 'Templates' section (see page 198). Bring your own little forest dweller to life and take it with you wherever you go!

Instructions

1. Decide which creature you like best in the 'Templates' section (see page 198).

2. Select a background fabric for the front.

3. Use your favourite stitches to bring it to life.

4. Once you have finished the front, select another piece of fabric for the back and sew the two together, leaving a small opening for stuffing.

5. Once stuffed and sewn up, your forest dweller is complete!

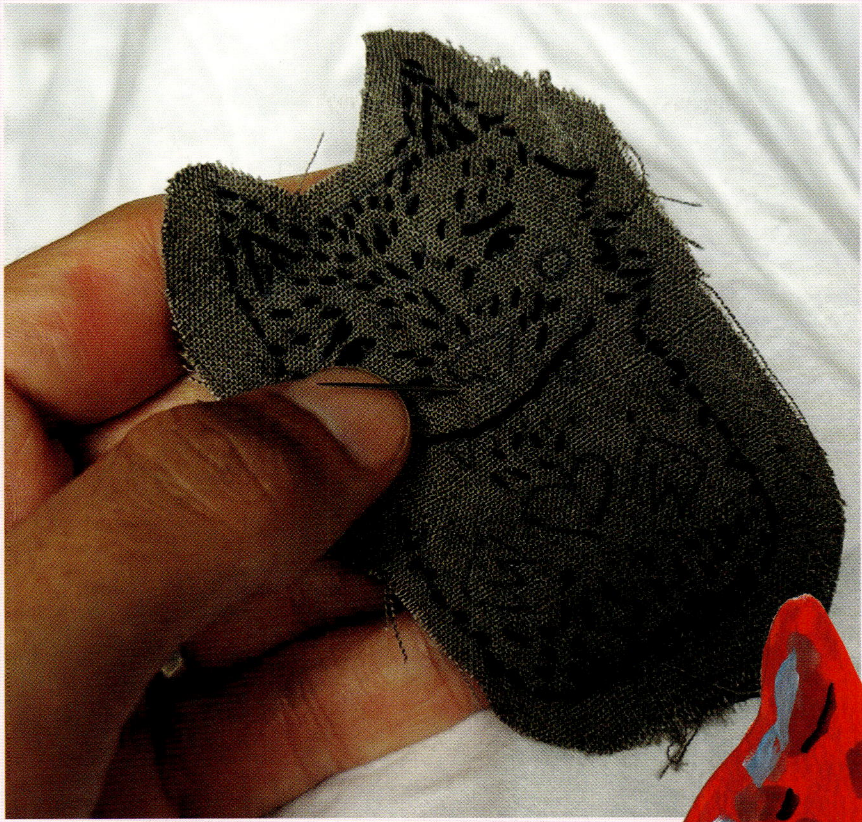

Use scraps of fabric to create your forest dwellers. It is a simple way of making use of little bits of material and giving them new life.

501
VALIENTE
JUSTO
FELIZ
DAME
TU
LUZ
De siempre
para
siempre
LET
LOVE
IN.
Hacia LA LUZ

Mend and customize

Without a doubt, the most sustainable clothing is that which we already have in our wardrobes. Sometimes, a garment just needs a little patch, some mending or a customized detail to breathe new life into it.

We are living in a time of the most unprecedented textile consumerism in the history of humanity, and the planet is suffering as a result. Brands produce cheap clothing, using synthetic fabrics, in countries where workers are exploited, simply so that consumers in the West can continue to buy more clothes they do not need. This cycle is creating an irreversible imbalance.

Have you ever wondered how many miles your clothes have travelled to reach you, and the impact this has on the environment? If we were to probe a little more into the fabric and the labour used to produce some of the clothes in our wardrobes, we might well be shocked. The time has come to wake up. This battle can clearly only be won if we form a community in which we all do our share. This revolution is very simple: it involves ceasing to buy clothes from places where it is impossible to fathom how their garments can be sold at such low prices. No one is forcing us to buy; this is a peaceful revolution. No one needs new clothes every three months, as the displays of seasonal ranges would have us believe. This is a practice which generates mountains of appalling-quality garments at ridiculously low prices.

It is clearly better to have one pair of high-quality trousers and a pure wool sweater than a dozen poorly-made garments that are impossible to repair.

Nowadays, in the West, we keep more clothes in our wardrobes that we have never worn than ones that are torn or need mending. If we ask ourselves, or anyone around us, how many pairs of trousers, bags or T-shirts we have in our wardrobe, we would be hard pressed to know the answer. This is a clear symptom of the era of capitalism and rampant consumerism in which we live. This path has led the planet to a situation of extreme emergency and the reality of irreversible climate change.

I hope you will allow me a few words: for me, textile art is a beneficial tool for many reasons.

There is an ever-increasing community of people who are keen to learn how to repair or customize their clothes. I have seen it in my workshops: people leave delighted to have brought life back to a garment that had languished forgotten in their wardrobe or needed mending.

The type of embroidery I do is always inspired by darning stitches, which I use decoratively. I think these 'survival stitches', as I call them, are beautiful. I call them this because they are the ones we all know how to do, the ones that come naturally when we pick up a needle and thread; they are rough stitches that become more precise with practice. All over the world, different methods of mending have been applied to textiles, some more prescribed than others, but I believe there is always a poetic beauty to be found in these repairs.

In this section, you will find a collection of photos of garments that I have mended, customized or darned, sometimes using tools such as the darning egg shown above.

You can use any of the illustrations found in the 'Templates' section of this book (see pages 196–203) to decorate your clothes, or choose your preferred stitches from the 'Favourite stitches' section (see pages 184–185) to make your repairs.

In this photo, you can see a simple stitch that I use for mending. Sometimes, using a different fabric or colour to the piece that we are repairing can give it a special, unique look.

calma
Silencio.

Valiente
Justo
Feliz

Instructions

I always say that when the fabric you want to repair has a tear, you need to treat it like a wound.

1. First, clean it up, cutting away any damaged fabric.
2. Then, create a neat edge by hemming along both sides of the tear.
3. Finally, suture it, sewing the fabric together. For holes or bad tears, you may need to apply a patch. You can make these discreet but I prefer to flaunt my patches, embellishing them with stitches, words or motifs so they become a decorative feature.

I hope this section encourages you to go through your wardrobe and bring some of your clothes back to life. Give yourself some freedom and don't be too harsh on yourself. Above all, have fun – this is the most important factor in achieving a satisfactory result.

Brave
Fair
happy

DAME
TU
LUZ

Let
Love
in.

siempre
ara
empre

501

This example shows us how you can conceal a stubborn stain that is impossible to remove, by putting a patch, or multiple patches, over it.

This is my favourite stitch – running stitch (see page 185). It is simple, relaxing, freely worked and always gives a beautiful result.

How lo
is forever?
TRES BALAS
CALIDAD
PERABLE

For embroidering letters, it is better to use smaller stitches such as backstitch and finer yarn or thread such as pearl cotton, embroidery thread, darning or topstitching thread, which will ensure that the texts are legible.

be brave

Mini throws

What I enjoy most about sewing is the possibility of projects that I can do when I am on the go. These include small-scale textile pieces that I can work on anywhere: travelling by train, in the countryside under a tree or while I am waiting for someone. I like the fact that I don't need a large space to work in, or a lot of material to bring my creative ideas to fruition.

Creativity should depend as little as possible on money. This is why my mini throws are made from scraps I come across or that people give to me.

For me, 80 per cent of what makes a textile piece interesting is the colours and types of fabric used. In the photographs of these mini throws, you can see something that is a recurrent theme in my textile work: I always use natural materials, predominantly cotton, wool, linen and silk.

In addition, my stitches are very simple – only the type of thread and the colours change. I focus more on selecting the right materials and colours than on making virtuoso stitches. The stitch I use most is running stitch, which you will find in the 'Favourite stitches' section of this book (see pages 184–185).

In this project, you will see two types of mini throws: those made from remnants of different fabrics which I use as the background for my designs and phrases, and those based on a piece of fabric that I have come across somewhere. As you will see, there are mini throws featuring Alice in Wonderland, Little Red Riding Hood and Peter Pan, simply because I have used particular small scraps of printed fabric.

If you look closely, you will see that you do not need many different stitches in a textile piece. Often, the colour and material you work with are the most important factors.

If you would like to make a mini throw based on my drawings and phrases, you will find several ideas in the 'Templates' section on pages 196–203. They are all made in the same way.

Instructions

1. First find some fabric that you'd like to use as the background. It should not be too big – no more than 50 × 40cm (20 × 16in).

2. Choose some contrasting offcuts of fabric, each no bigger than 15 × 15cm (6 × 6in), and enough to cover most of the background material. You can select them on the basis of colour or texture, or even just to use up any remnants that you might have. In this way you are letting chance decide the aesthetic of your work! Anything goes.

3. Work your favourite stitches on these scraps, then add appliqué, buttons or pieces of lace. When it comes to a mini throw, if you like it, use it.

4. Then arrange all the pieces of decorated fabric on the background material. This is my favourite part: using pins to hold them in place, move them around as necessary until you are happy with the final look.

5. Once you have decided where they are all to go, sew them to the background material.

6. Your mini throw is complete!

You may have already started to see those forlorn scraps of material in a very different light. They might include pieces left over from a larger textile project, an old T-shirt you no longer wear, or buttons from a torn shirt that has a certain sentimental value. Cover your mini throws with fabrics that hold a special significance to you.

When you are working at such a small scale, you will find that even if you do need to buy some fabric, you will need very little. If you have fallen in love with a particular design, you will only need a small amount for it to feature in your project.

Mini throws are perfect for hanging on the wall, using as the front of a bag, making into an attractive cushion or simply having about to generally brighten up your life. And they definitely make the perfect gift for your nearest and dearest.

People often ask me when I know my mini throws are finished. Normally, there is no such thing as 'finished', because it would be possible to go on adding things forever. So, the answer is to listen for when your intuition tells you it is time to declare your project complete.

Le
petit
textile
Depuis
1983
a.saraiba

I hope these details inspire you and give you ideas for future work. Notice the freedom with which the fabrics are cut into shapes and the stitches formed.

Note the different types of fabric you can see in this photo: they include lace, vintage bedspreads and pieces of linen and cotton. This is how I achieve the textures that give my work its character.

Once again, notice the simplicity of the stitching. Have fun and enjoy the freedom of your fabrics.

Sometimes
just one
second.

In the photos here and on the previous and following pages you can see how I arrange the pieces of fabric and the result after I have worked over them in various stitches including running stitch and whip stitch.

never
grow
up

amour.
BARCELONA

Scatter cushions

Fabrics can also be used to make items for the home. Here is one of my favourite examples: a scatter cushion. My house is full of cushions, but for some reason it never feels like enough. Whether for reading, while I sew, or during a siesta with my dogs, I always feel that the more cushions around me, the better. When we make textile art for everyday life, it always seems to make life more beautiful.

For this cushion, I used remnants that were lying around my workshop, selecting a range of browns and ochres. First I worked each square that would make up the front of the cushion, then I sewed the four parts together to make a single piece.

I used a different technique on each of them: on one I used *boro* patching; on another, an appliqué heart: I embroidered the word *amour* on the third; and on the last, I liked the flower print so much that I simply added a couple of patches to hide the tears in it.

As you may have noticed, my main aim with this book is to offer you inspiration for your own work. This cushion is a good summary of the various different techniques I have suggested on the previous pages. Feel free to use them and combine them in any way you want.

Instructions

1. Decide which fabrics you will join together to make the front.

2. Decorate them using different techniques (*boro*, appliqué, etc.). You will find a wide variety of illustrations in the 'Templates' section of the book (see pages 196–203).

3. Sew them all together into a single piece that will form the front of your cushion.

4. Choose a fabric for the back.

5. Sew the front to the back leaving a gap of at least 10cm (4in) so you can stuff. The stuffing could be an old pillow, wool or fabric remnants.

6. Once you have finished stuffing, sew up the opening.

a. saraiva

Appliqué

Appliqué is possibly one of my favourite techniques. It is simple and the result is stunning. It is also very pictorial: in doing appliqué work you can take inspiration from a whole gamut of things including paintings, regional costumes and ceramic designs. In this section I have included various photographs of *La Vijanera*, a pagan festival celebrated in the Cantabria region of Spain, Portuguese tiles, and others that I have taken over the years and during the journeys that have inspired the majority of my textile work. I hope they inspire you as much as they did me.

This technique is perfect for adding personality to bedspreads and quilts, or for creating large pieces to use as wall hangings.

For the background, use a tough fabric that won't be pulled out of shape by what is sewn onto it. For the appliqué, I have often used old blankets made of pure wool – these are a great option because they are easy to cut and there is no danger that the edges will fray. Another possibility is merino-wool felt which is my favourite material for these projects. It is often used to make Spanish regional costumes and is undoubtedly the best option for doing appliqué.

Old scarves and sweaters are another good choice, particularly any that have felted after an accidental hot wash: the resulting texture makes them perfect for cutting up.

On one occasion, moths got at several of my woollen sweaters. I washed them at maximum temperature in the washing machine so they would shrink and felt, turning them into excellent material for use in my appliqué. One good trick for felting wool is to subject it to sudden temperature changes, such as taking it out of a high-temperature wash and plunging it into a bowl of cold water. This can do a fair bit of the felting for you. Obviously, this advice is for clothes that you no longer wish to use. These techniques are terrible for clothes that do still have some life in them, but great if you no longer want to wear them and are happy to use them for appliqué projects.

Feel free to make the bedspread as large or small as you need. I always use an old blanket as the background.

If you don't have any of these fabrics to hand, don't worry. Once more, use whatever you have. Sometimes, two fine pieces of material can work for appliqué if you use one as the backing. Linen and cotton definitely go well together. In this case, the only thing you need to do differently is to hem the appliqué so it doesn't fray. This is particularly important if it is an item that is going to be used on a daily basis.

However, if you will be using it as a wall hanging, you don't need to worry about hemming the shapes you have cut out.

One option for attaching appliqué shapes is to embroider directly on them or on the background fabric. In many of these photos you can see appliqué on which I have embroidered different patterns to add additional textures to the piece.

Instructions

1. Decide which fabric you will use as the background.
2. Choose the material from which you will cut out the appliqué shapes.
3. Arrange the appliqué shapes on the background fabric and hold in place with pins.
4. Sew the shapes to the background fabric.
5. Your work is complete!

Whenever I go to local festivals near the village where I live in Spain, I take photographs of the regional costumes and other small details. These end up being a great source of inspiration for my textile works.

valiente.

sin miedo

I took this photograph at the pagan celebration of *La Vijanera*. The costumes worn as part of European pagan celebrations will always be a central theme of my work.

Hello

Textile books

One of my favourite things to do with forgotten fabrics, old buttons or little charms is to make them into textile books. I combine in them all the materials that are stored in little boxes in my studio: things I have kept because they caught my fancy and which find companions in my free-form compositions.

For me, a textile book is one of the nicest portable artworks ever invented by humans. Their simple yet undeniably effective design has ensured their survival over the centuries. Transferring design concepts that we associate with paper to textiles is a job that I really enjoy.

I usually start with a background fabric that I use to make the pages. I then create compositions with remnants that are too small to be useful for larger-scale work. In this way, little buttons and scraps of cloth are rescued from obscurity and given new dignity, once sorted, ironed and carefully sewn onto the pages of the book.

I generally use old bedspreads to make the cover. I like them because they are wadded which gives the book a bit more of a solid feel. If you haven't got an old bedspread to hand, you can always make a cover with some nice vintage fabric, sandwiched around a piece of old blanket, a towel, or any material that will give the cover the firmness you desire.

For me, textile books are like scapulars: I keep adding things and rarely think of them as complete. These are projects on which I can continue to work over time.

For example, I might find a lamb-shaped pendant on the street that would be perfect for some work that I had begun months or years previously.

As you can see, there is room for everything in these little textile books, and you can keep on working on them for as long you want.

Instructions

1. Choose the fabric you want to use for the pages of your book. This fabric should be double the width of the final size that you want the book to be.

2. On this strip of fabric, arrange your pieces of printed, dyed or vintage material, along with the buttons, beads and other bits and bobs you want to use to decorate it.

3. When you have finished decorating, fold this cloth in half and sew together as shown on page 134; this will give you two double-sided pages of the book.

4. Now fold your pages in half again. You can make as many pages as you like. Tie them together with ribbon (see the illustration on page 134).

5. Decide which fabric you want to use for the cover. It could be a piece of an old bedspread, so it is a bit thicker and gives the book more stability. If you don't have a bedspread, use whatever fabric you like, adding a piece of old blanket or towel for wadding (batting). Fold and sew together as you did for the pages.

6. Once the pages are finished, sew a ribbon to the cover of the book so you can tie the book closed.

7. Sew the ribbons securing your pages from step 4 to the spine of the cover to hold it in place. And there you have it! Enjoy decorating the cover or adding details such as those you can see in the photos in this section.

Instructions for textile book

1–2

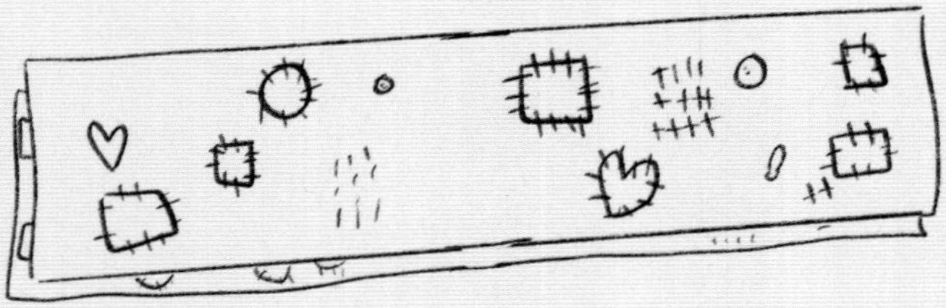

Add decorations to your pages – these will be folded in half, so make sure they are wide enough.

3 Once the decorations are sewn on, fold these pieces of fabric in half and sew together.

Make a 1cm (½in) hem.

4 Fold these strips in half again to make the pages of your book.

Tie them together with a piece of ribbon; this will be the inside of your book.

5–6 Now sew the cover fabric to the wadding (batting).

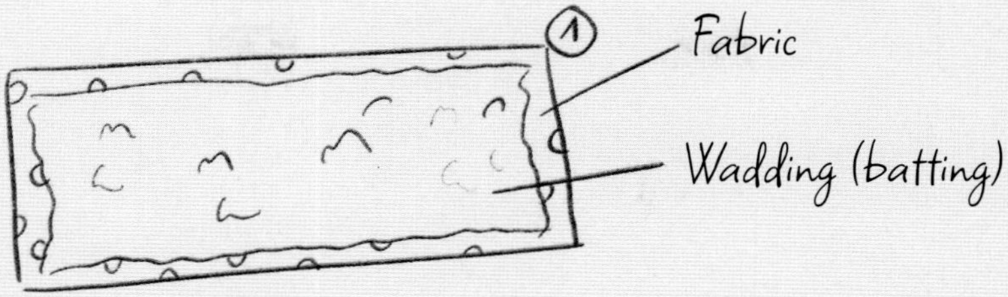

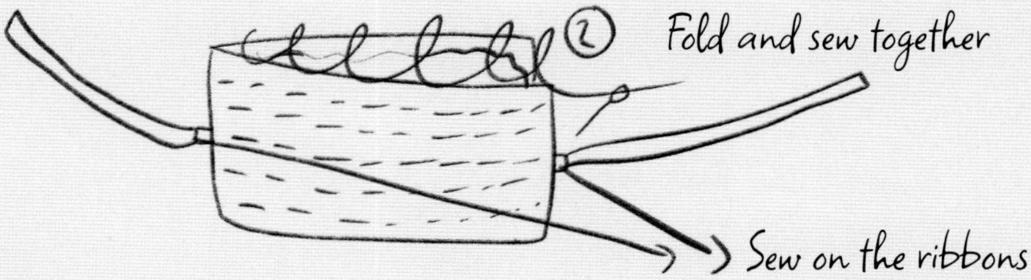

7

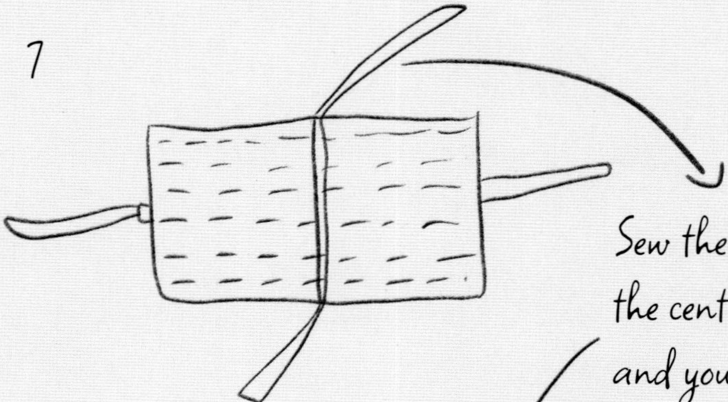

Sew the ribbon from step 4 in the centre, insert your pages and your book is complete.

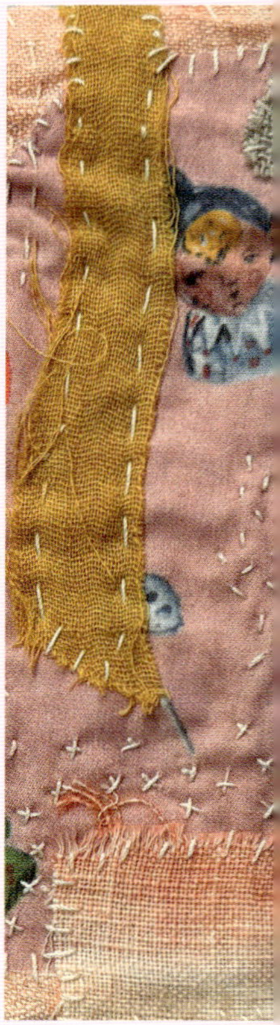

A
A a

Snippet rolls

As you have seen, many of the textile projects I suggest are small-scale and a number can be easily carried with you. Of all of them, the ones that best embody these principles are my 'snippet rolls'.

You can see from the photographs the number of different fabrics and yarns that I combine on the strips, which I wind round a cylindrical wooden clothes peg that goes everywhere with me.

I love meditative, free sewing; stitching for the love of the needle, the thread, the texture and the feeling of peace that it engenders in me. My snippet rolls come with me on trains, buses and planes: a little needle and a small amount of thread are enough to turn any place into a studio.

Sewing has never taken up much space in history, in any sense, yet it has always been present: old biscuit tins for instance, holding the personal and creative universes of the people who fill them with the little treasures that will later be sewn or embroidered.

For my snippet rolls, I always use fabric from old sheets that I colour with natural dyes. I then work using a wide variety of wool, silk, linen or cotton threads to create different textures and relief.

I also use a lot of scraps of printed fabric, even tiny patches, which end up in my snippet rolls.

Instructions

1. Find a wooden clothes peg, a chopstick or any other cylindrical rod around which you can wind your snippet roll.

2. Cut the fabric you are going to use as the background. I usually use strips of fabric 7cm (2¾in) in width and 120cm (48in) in length, but these measurements are for guidance only. Adjust these according to your own requirements.

(3) Start sewing your favourite stitches freestyle onto your snippet roll. Perhaps one might be a travel journal, while another could be memories of a loved one, for whom it would make a delightful present. The possibilities are infinite.

miedo.
Calma.

prueba #1
prueba #3
prueba #4
SWISS MADE
FERBY
LYRA

Block printing

Woodcut or block printing is a very simple stamping technique that allows us to print our own designs onto fabric.

If you have never tried block printing, there are kits available, such as the one by Fábrica de Texturas, which are perfect for getting started with this wonderful technique.

In terms of the simplest and cheapest tools, offering good value for money, the lino cutters made by ESSDEE are a very good option for beginners, as are their flexible printing blocks, fabric inks and rubber rollers. The materials are easy to find.

Before starting, I would recommend you do a trial run on a printing block to see what type of cut each of the cutters makes. You will quickly start to see the differences between them, and discover which ones are best for the shapes you want for your design.

Iron the fabric that you are going to print on so it is stretched nice and flat, and before stamping the design onto it, do a practice run on a piece of paper so you are sure the design is to your liking.

I usually jot the print number down on a piece of paper, and if I change the design I put the new one next to it, numbering the trials before I start printing directly onto the fabric.

Only apply a small amount of ink when using the roller. An error that we all make at the beginning is putting too much ink on our stamping block.

If your designs are small, such as squares, circles or abstract shapes, you can make your own textile stamps with them. Start by making simple designs until you become more skilled with the materials, and then you can move on to more complex designs.

Instructions

1. Draw your designs onto the printing block. You can use any of the many designs contained in this book (see pages 196–203).

2. Use the lino cutter to remove the parts of the design that you do not want to be inked. Remember that the final result will be a negative of your carving.

3. Using a rubber roller and textile ink, stamp the pattern you have created onto your old remnants and favourite fabrics.

4. You can combine as many pieces of fabric and prints as you like.

5. Finally, sew the pieces together with a freestyle running stitch (see page 185).

NATURAL

dyes

Natural dyes have been an essential process in all my textile work. The idea of using what at first could be seen as waste products, such as avocado skins or onion peelings, to colour old pieces of fabric, is akin to alchemy for me. It is a process I consider just as important as embroidering or working on the cloth in other ways.

The colours obtained from natural dyes have end results and shades that cannot be replicated by any other type of dye. They are magical.

When they see one of my pieces, many people ask how they can do something similar, or why, even though they have tried, they have not achieved the desired result. I always advise them to try to create colours naturally, because when we create our own range of colours from natural dyes, our work is enriched.

In my textile work, I nearly always place more importance on the process and the materials than on the technique, especially the way in which these materials are obtained. It is not a matter of going to a shop and buying them, but rather rooting around in old fabric shops and markets, and rummaging through old family wardrobes. It's about creating colours from plants, vegetables, fruit and roots.

If you use natural dyes, colours can turn out one way on a particular day, and another way the next, or fabrics might react in different ways, giving totally different results. This alchemy of the creative process interests me much more than the final result of the piece.

In this section, I have taken the liberty of setting out some recipes and processes covering simple ways of making natural dyes.

There are many books on natural dyeing, but my advice is just to give it a go. This will give you a basic handle on the process. The water, plants or fruit that you use will give different results depending on their origin. The best approach is to experiment, enjoy the process and get stuck into investigating which dye plants grow in your area. If you wish to continue researching dyes, you will find many methods, recipes and processes for achieving different colours.

Take this chapter as a mini-introduction to the world of colour that I find so fascinating. I hope that this little guide to natural dyes inspires you to create your first colour palettes.

Logwood (Campeche)

This is widely seen as one of the simplest dyes. Campeche wood is native to Mesoamerica, but has been used in Europe for centuries as a textile dye.

You can use it to achieve colours ranging from lilac to deep purple, depending on the amount of water and dye you add. To begin, add water and a little logwood to a small saucepan. Heat, but do not allow to boil. You will soon see how the water turns to a shade somewhere between lilac and purple.

When making dyes, it is important not to use saucepans or bowls that you will use later for cooking. Additionally, natural dyes only work properly on natural materials, such as cotton, silk, linen or wool. The material should be soaked before it is dipped in the dye bath to make the fibres more permeable to colour.

You can take the saucepan off the heat before you submerge the material. Leave it soaking for anywhere between ten minutes and a full day. You will get different results and shades with each experiment. The length of time you leave the material in the dye will depend on the colour you wish to achieve. Obviously the longer you leave it and the more dye you use, the darker the shade will be. Make use of this little guide to play around and experiment.

When the material is dyed the colour you want, remove it from the dye bath and immerse it in another saucepan containing water heated with alum. Alum is the mordant I use to fix the colours, as it is a natural mineral that is easy to find and inexpensive. Alum prevents colours from fading and makes the tones a bit brighter. I usually add alum equal to one-tenth of the material's weight. Finally, rinse well and leave the dyed material to dry naturally in the shade.

Tea

The first dye that I made was with black tea. Tea formed part of my daily routine and I had it with my breakfast every morning. We have all noticed the colour that wet teabags leave behind when we take them out of the mug, so without really knowing what I was doing, one day I decided to scale up this effect. It is still one of my favourite dye colours. The ochres, golds and browns obtained from tea are unique.

It is best to do a few test runs in a small saucepan to determine the colour proportions. You can use tea bags, simply as they come, or put loose tea in a cotton bag as I do, so that the colour can easily infuse the water.

Bring the water and tea to the boil, leave it to steep for a while, then remove the tea to allow the colour to settle. I find it helpful to store it in a cool, dark place for a day after taking it off the heat.

When you are ready to use it, heat the dye solution again, without allowing it to boil, and submerge the material that you are dyeing. Experiment with small offcuts and different submersion times to find out what shades you can achieve. Finally, to fix the colour, follow the instructions given in the 'Logwood' section (see page 156).

Cochineal

The best cochineal is to be found in the Canary Islands. Canaturex, a company specializing in cochineal farming, has been working for decades to use the most appropriate, ethical processes.

Grind the cochineal, leave it to soak overnight, and the next day it will be ready to add to a pan of simmering water. You can put the cochineal in a little cotton bag to avoid uneven patches of colour on the fabric or, if you prefer that effect, allow the fabric to take on different shades from pink to red. To fix the colour, follow the instructions in the 'Logwood' section (see page 156).

Enjoy the variety of colours, which range from pink to red. The results are surprising.

Natural dyes are amazing for achieving the full range of shades of a particular colour, from lightest to darkest. Don't just use your dyes once – to take full advantage of them, you should continue to use them until they stop producing any colour.

CANATUREX
EL SECRETO DE LA COCHINILLA
AZOR o CARTAMO
AMARILLO.
MATERIAL: LANA, ALGODÓN
MORDEDURA PREVIA: NO
AMARILLO ANARANJADO.
MATERIAL: LANA.
MORDEDURA PREVIA: SI

Onion

This is one of the most surprising dyes that I have come across. The first time I used it, I felt the natural magic of alchemy. I never throw away onion peel any more. The fact that something that used to go in the bin now plays a very significant role in my work is something that fascinates me about textile processes.

You will not need any mordant (colour fixative) to achieve the yellow obtained from onion skin.

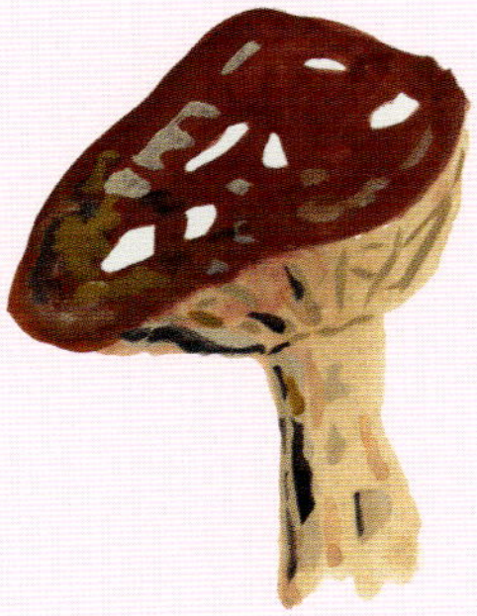

Add all the onion skins you can to a saucepan of water and bring to the boil. After a few minutes, you will see the water turning yellow. As with the other dyes we have looked at, the more onion skins you use, the darker the shade will be. Simply follow the instructions on page 156 but skip the stage of using alum as you don't need a mordant.

Iron

This is one of the simplest processes – even easier than any of the previous dyes we have looked at – and we can use it to achieve darker colours. Using this recipe, you can even get the colour black.

Note: it is particularly important with this dye that none of the saucepans or bowls used during the dye process are used subsequently for cooking. In addition, you must always wear gloves during the process.

The recipe is simple: put a handful of nails, two glasses of water and a glass of white vinegar in a jar (do not put the lid on, because natural gases are given off during the process). Leave the jar outside but protected from the elements for at least a week.

Once this time has passed, using gloves and with the help of a pair of tongs, immerse the fabric to be dyed in the iron solution. You need only submerge it in the liquid for a few minutes, without heating. Afterwards, rinse well in clear water, still wearing the gloves.

The results are remarkable. Once the fabric has been thoroughly rinsed and dried, you can use it without any problem. You can repeat the process as many times as you like, using the same nails.

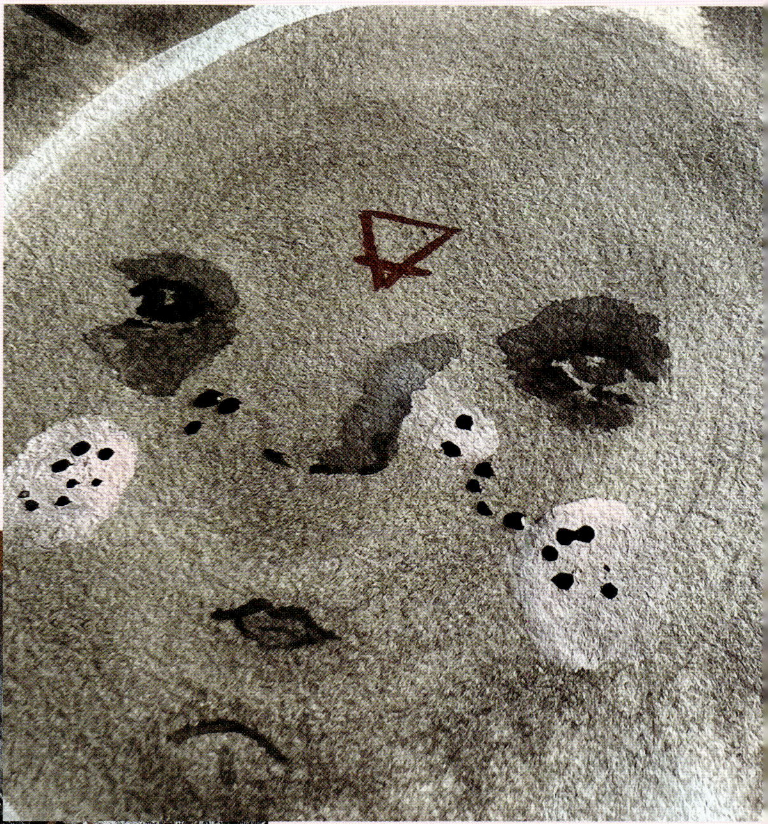

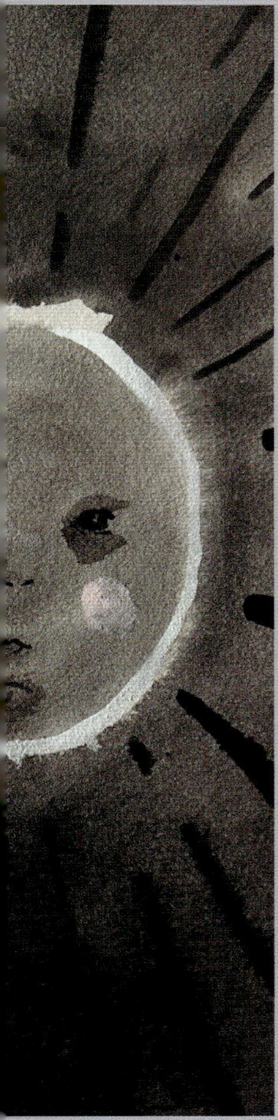

SEWING

materials

1
MERCHANT & MILLS
A TIDY AMOUNT
FINE BLACK SAFETY PINS
Carolyn N.K. Denham
DRESSES COURSES PATTERNS NOTIONS
2
3
4
MERCHANT & MILLS
100
SIZE 2 BLACK ENAMELLED
ENTOMOLOGY PINS
FOR EXTRA FINE FABRICS
Carolyn N.K. Denham
DRESSES COURSES PATTERNS NOTIONS
5
Cohana
MADE IN JAPAN
6
7
8
9
10
11
12

Tools

1. **Safety pins** – always useful for any textile process.

2. **Thimbles.** There are many different types, from traditional European to Japanese styles.

3. **Needle holders.** Very useful for transporting your prized needles easily and ensuring they don't get mislaid.

4. **Pins.** I very much like the British brand Merchant & Mills. It is important to have plenty of pins as they bring things to life right from the start of a project; you can see the composition and end result much earlier in the process.

5. A good **pair of scissors** is always essential in a textile workshop. It is preferable to have one good pair solely for cutting fabric than several lesser-quality pairs. They should not be used to cut anything other than fabric.

6. **Round-ended scissors** for cutting thread.

7. **Beeswax.** I use it for waxing gold threads or others that are difficult to work with.

8. **Thread cutter.** A great tool for getting rid of any thread tails.

9. **Embroidery hoop.** I only use these for fabrics where necessary.

10. **Needle sharpener** from the Japanese brand Cohana. When you have high-quality needles, it is great to be able to prolong their lives by sharpening them.

11. **Mini loom.** You can use this to create fabric for your projects.

12. **Travel scissors.** The best ones I have found are from the Japanese brand Cohana. You can take them with you on trains, buses and planes without any problem.

1
2
3
#8
WonderFil
Perle Cotton
212
5g
4
5
6
7
#8
WonderFil
Perle Cotton
EZM1046
5g
8
9
10
11

Threads

1. **Vintage threads of all types.** I use these a lot in my work. They are more liable to break, but you can use them for small details and they add character to your work.

2. This **strong, shiny thread** from GlaMore™ has a very professional finish and is available in many colours from Wonderfil.

3. For *boro* work, **pearl cotton** is one of my favourites. I usually use number 8, but there are several thicknesses on the market, so you will easily find one that suits your style.

4. **Dazzle™** is a tough, metallic thread that is perfect for details. Wonderfil has a lovely range of colours.

5. This **pearl cotton thread**, Eleganza™ by Wonderfil, has incredible variegated shades.

6. **Wool** from my sheep, hand-dyed at home using natural plant dyes. I love the effect of its matte finish on embroidery.

7. Another **pearl cotton**. In this case the colour gradients lend a very special touch to the finished piece.

8. **Japanese cotton thread** for *boro*, *sashiko* and darning; always in my sewing box.

9. **Egyptian cotton thread**, ideal for working small details. This one is from Wonderfil and is very strong.

10. **Linen thread.** My top choice when I want to give my work a timeless, vintage look.

11. **Merino wool yarn**, hand-dyed at home.

FAVOURITE

stitches

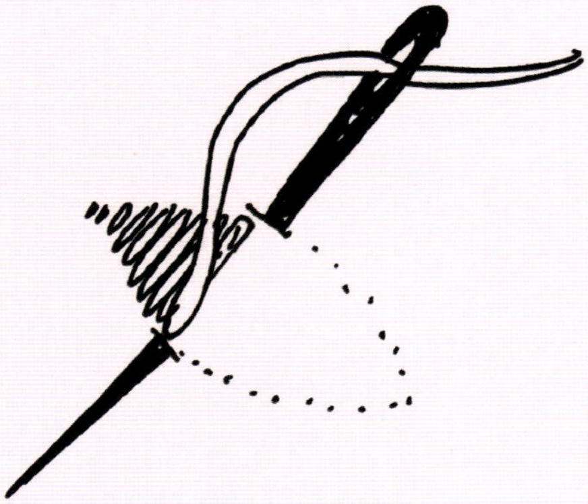

Satin stitch

Perfect for embroidery, if there are areas of the design you want to fill.

Seed stitch

These are freestyle stitches. Also known as 'slow stitching'. You will find clear examples of this stitch in the 'Mend and customize' section (see page 71).

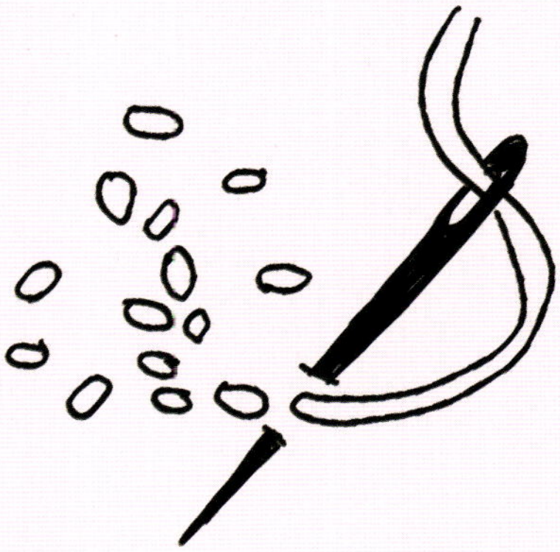

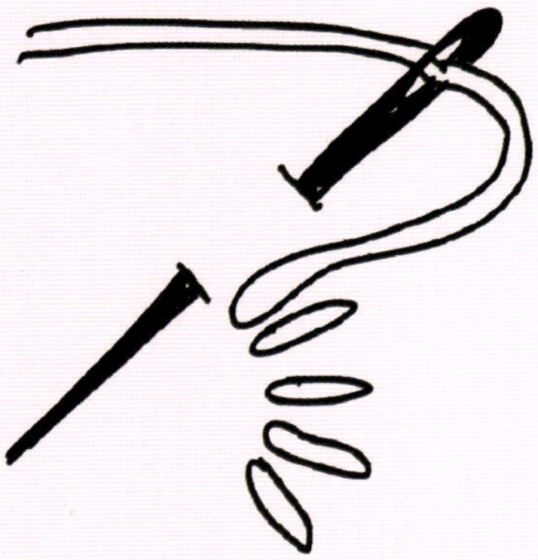

Straight stitch

This type of stitch is perfect for embroidering flowers or branches.

Stem stitch

This is one of the stitches that I use the most. You will find examples of it in both the photos and the pattern of the *Boro* project (see page 43).

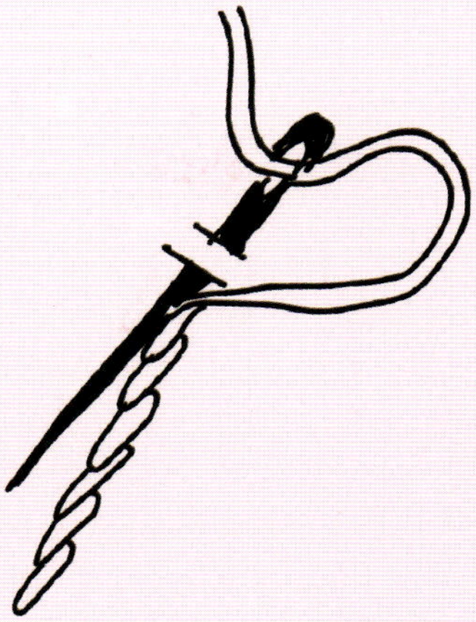

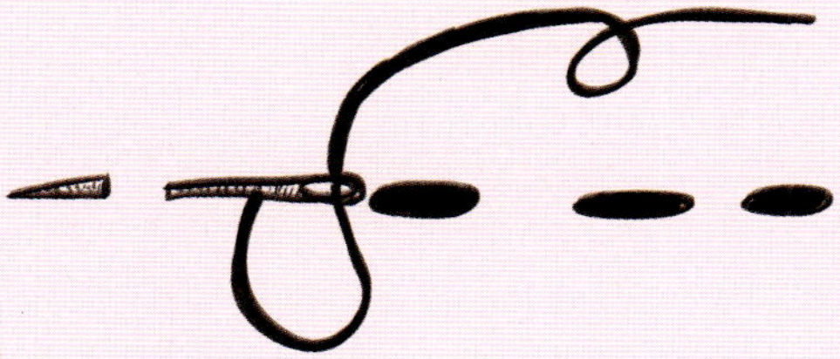

Running stitch

This stitch is one of the simplest and most widely used in the projects in this book and indeed in all my work. You will find examples right across the different projects that I suggest, including the *Boro* project.

Whip stitch

Perfect for joining fabrics together and sewing appliqué to the background, or for attaching patches.

EPILOGUE

Lana Robla

By way of conclusion to this overview of my textile techniques and inspirations, I could not finish without this chapter, which perhaps summarizes all my work over the last 20 years.

Lana Robla is my personal project to save the wool of the valley in which I live, in the Cantabria region of Spain. The tragedy of considering it a waste product is widely known, and having the opportunity to save this wonderful material gifted to us by nature has become central to my life.

Living a life connected with the land we inhabit is a thread that has run throughout the different sections and projects in this book. In my case, I live in a stone house in a valley, far from everything, with a spring as our only source of drinking water and firewood to keep ourselves warm in winter. Not only does this region boast amazing wild strawberries and wonderful elderberries, but its sheep form a fundamental part of our ecosystem. Without these sheep, who live freely in the valley, the vegetation would grow so high that the houses would disappear and the danger of fires would be even greater. This is the vital role they play. Dignifying the wool of these sheep is one of my life's goals.

Wool is much stigmatized, especially when it is not as soft and silky as the textile industry expects. After travelling the world, speaking to shepherds and studying the traditional costumes of different regions, it has become clear to me that each sheep is specific to its territory to provide a particular type of wool which, as a fabric, contributes to human survival.

As in so many areas of the planet, the animals roam freely in the mountains around the valley where I live. They interbreed – a process in which standards are of little importance; what is essential is that the animals remain healthy and attuned to the local climate. It is their wool that has sustained the most harm, because these animals have been politicized with subsidies, nationalism and breed standards imposed by humans, never by nature. This is the wool that we have in the valley where I live, from sheep that have crossbred with each other, oblivious to all of the above. It is the wool that we have, and the wool that I am trying to save.

Without them, we would be nothing.

Some fibres are coarser, others are softer; some are perfect for making thick felts that protect us from the rain; others will be used for fine socks for babies, or thick sweaters to keep us warm when we are working in very cold places. All wools are useful; we just have to find what for.

My *Lana Robla* project would be impossible without the help of my friend Josito. He is one of my neighbours in the valley where I live, together with another 93 inhabitants, over a land area not much smaller than many cities, but which is home to only around 40 families.

We started by gathering wool from Josito's flock of 15 and have ended up collecting it from 400 sheep in the valley, whose wool had been going straight to landfill prior to this point. This is why I said at the beginning that this chapter sums up the philosophy behind my work and what I have tried to convey in this book.

I make all the colours of our wool by hand, using natural dyes. Spinning is done in two different ways: by hand using a spindle and spinning wheel, and by the Wool Dreamers project in Cuenca.

I have found various successful outlets for our wool; it is used to make hand-knitted work socks, as well as skeins of embroidery yarn.

Maybe in the region where you live, there is some textile or fibre waste waiting to be saved and its dignity restored. I believe that the moment has come for us to sit up and listen to what the Earth has been telling us for so long: everything that we need is already here, we need nothing more.

Please excuse this chapter, which for me is the most pertinent in this book; a book in which art has led me to explore my creative process in so many different directions. But the most rewarding part of my journey of artistic expression through textile work has been delving into the materials and their origins.

My journey of discovery in the world of wool, enshrined in the heart of my textile work, has been one of the most precious gifts life has given me.

I hope the pages of this book will fuel your creativity with endless inspiration and help you connect with your region and your way of being on this beautiful planet.

LANA ROBLA
39696
CANTABRIA
VALLES PASIEGOS

TEMPLATES

oak
Silencio
Silence
Let love in.
craftman

a. saraiba

ADDITIONAL TEMPLATES

The Swan

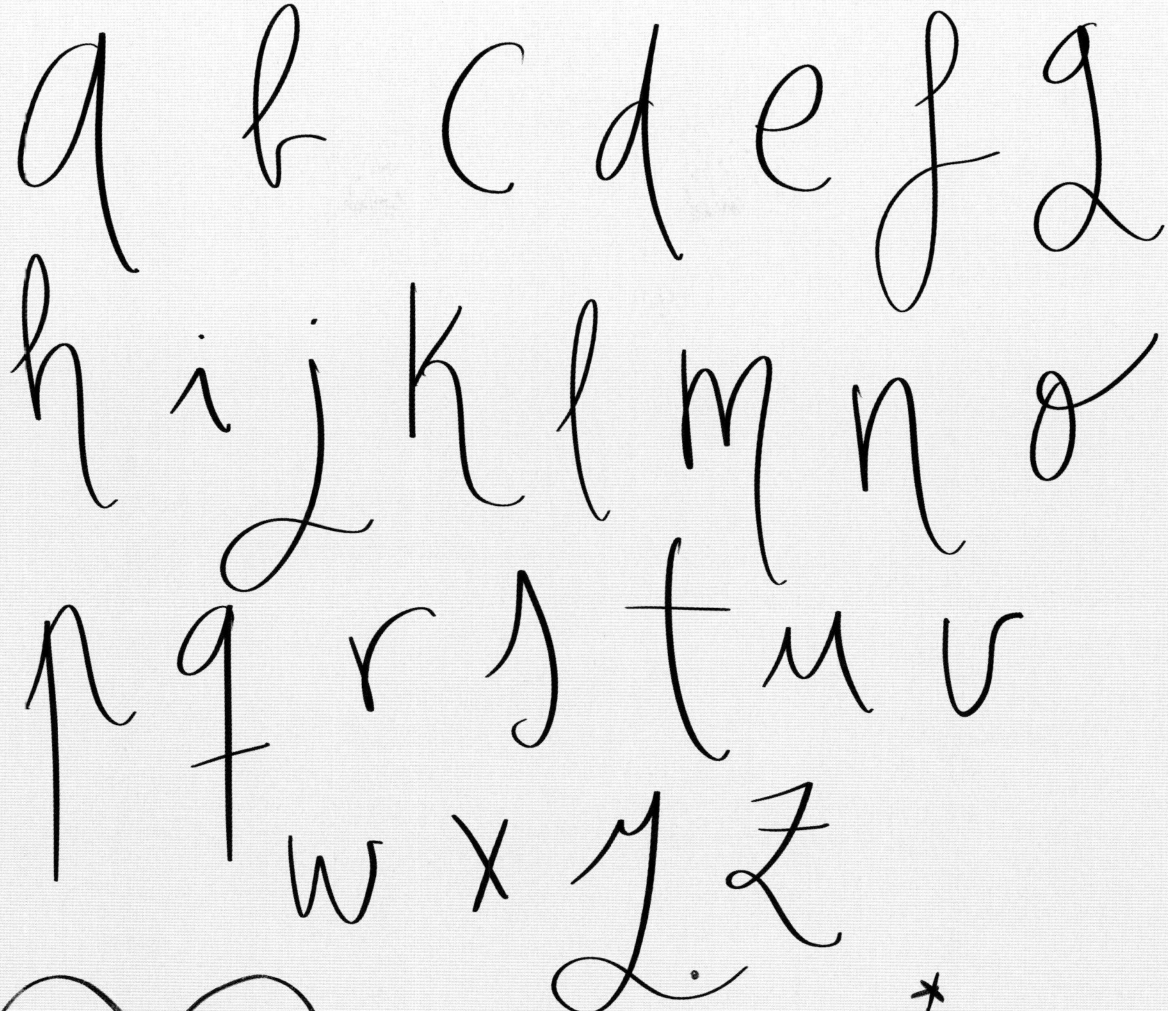

Eternal love

Sewing

Eternal love

Live life

Fearless

ABBAYE DE FLAVIGNY - BONBONS A LA ROSE
FLAVIGNY ABBEY - ROSE CANDIES FLAVORED
Sin
miedo